the West Highland White Terrier

A guide to selection, care, nutrition, upbringing, training, health, breeding, sports and play.

Contents

Foreword

The book you are holding is a basic 'owner's manual'
for everyone owning a West Highland White Terrier
and also for those who are considering buying a
West Highland White Terrier. What we have done in
this book is to give the information to help the (future)
owner of a West Highland White Terrier look after
his or her pet responsibly. Too many people still buy
a pet before really understanding what they're about
to get into.

This book goes into the broad history of the West
Highland White Terrier, the breed standard and
some pros and cons of buying a West Highland
White Terrier. You will also find essential information
on feeding, initial training and an introduction in
reproduction. Finally we give attention to (day-to-day)
care, health and some breed-specific ailments.

Based on this information, you can buy a West
Highland White Terrier, having thought it through
carefully, and keep it as a pet in a responsible manner.
Our advice, though, is not just to leave it to this small
book. A properly brought-up and well-trained dog is
more than just a dog. Invest a little extra in a puppy
training course or an obedience course. There are also
excellent books available that go deeper into certain
aspects than is possible here.

About Pets

A Publication of About Pets.

Copyright © 2005
About Pets
co-publisher United Kingdom
Kingdom Books
PO9 5TL, England

ISBN 1852791985
First printing September 2003
Second printing May 2005

Original title: *de West Highland white terriër*
© 2002-2005 Welzo Media Productions bv,
About Pets,
Warffum, the Netherlands
http://www.aboutpets.info

Photos:
Rob Dekker, Rob Doolaard, N. te Boekhorst-
Henrix, H.T. Stavenga, Anja Romberg, Nicole
Michiels, Ilse Blankesteijn, Jose Spiek
and members of the West Highland
White Terrier Club

Printed in China

In General

Just like most short-legged Terriers, Westies still unite in themselves all the character traits they have ever needed to do the job of pest controllers.

The fascinating aspect of the Westie's character is the combination of lively spontaneity, perseverance (whatever it's got into its head, you'll find difficult to get out), toughness, restraint, pluck, affection and also sensitivity to its loved ones, which might even include the cat of the house. There are Westies that live happily together with Siamese cats or ordinary house cats. Its own cat is its friend, but that doesn't mean it won't eagerly chase other cats outdoors. A well-socialised Westie is busy, happy and self-assured. This is not a dog for just one person, but a dog for the whole family, especially as its love of running comes into its own as a family dog. A Westie is in its element on the move, in woods and fields. However do remember that lawns will undergo treatment that will raise the garden lover's hair, including the digging up of (imaginary) prey. As the Westie's housemate, you have to be able to understand that, because a Westie that's been out digging in wet weather will look the worse for wear after a while. Whole clumps of grass and earth get pulled out while it's digging and some Westies come home from a walk looking more than a little dishevelled. Many Westie owners often have to put up with other people saying "I think it's time you bathed your dog madam, the beast is black!". This is not what's needed (the bathtub that is), but we'll come back on that later. One of the aspects of the Westie's temperament is its lusty bark. This can help if you're worried about burglars. Some males can produce such a bark that, if you didn't know it was a Westie, you would think it was a good-sized dog. Their ancestors needed such a bark to announce that they sensed prey, and thus it was functional. Unfortunately, barking is not something we place much value on in today's society, so a Westie needs a rigorous upbringing. This doesn't need to be harsh as such, more subtle but consistent. You'll need the perseverance of a Westie! Every description of the breed has a word of warning for those who, in the first instance, fall in love with the West Highland White Terrier's looks. But its appearance (especially in 'show trim') says little about what the Westie is really all about. The show trim with its 'chrysanthemum' head gives an impression of softness, pliability, docility, calm and humbleness. You're in for a major surprise if you think that a Westie's temperament is like that of other pretty, white dogs (a poodle or a small bichon, for instance). Don't fall into that trap. Furthermore, a Westie at home or on a walk will never look as perfect as those Westies in dog shows.

Origins
The Westie is one of the group of Terriers and, more specifically, of the group of so-called short-legged Terriers. The short-legged Terriers are distinguished from their compatriots, the long-legged

Terriers, by the length of their legs relative to their body. Thus the Yorkshire Terrier, despite being smaller than the Westie, the Cairn, the Skye, the Norwich and the Norfolk Terriers (to name just a few) is actually a long-legged breed. The short-legged Terriers are literally 'low on their legs'.

These are ground working dogs (the name 'Terrier' comes from the Latin: terra = earth), and they were originally bred to fight pests. That meant they had to track down undesirable animals (often above and under the ground), and that they had to be the match of their opponents, and be able to make short meat of them. If you look at a list of their prey, you will realise that they needed a not inconsiderable portion of courage, toughness, and perseverance if they were going to do the job expected of them. Foxes, otters, badgers and rats were on the agenda, and a good terrier needed all its special characteristics if it were to be up to the job. Today's Terriers are still like that, although a layman, looking at their outward appearance and the appeal they beam out, might not think so. The toughness these dogs needed certainly came from the strict selection for functionality rather than attractiveness. A badger would be put in a barrel and a dog added. If the badger was killed, then the dog was considered as adequate. If the dog wound up

badly bitten or even dead itself, then it was 'de-selected'. It sounds rather drastic, but that is what is known to have happened. The Westie's origins are in Scotland, and to many people it is best known as that sweet little white dog on the famous whisky label. If you drive through Scotland's imposing but barren landscape, with the coarse architecture of its small farms and crofts, look at the country around you and imagine how bad weather could test the land, man and animals. Then you can also imagine that dogs were needed here that were purely functional as working dogs, with no ceremony. After all, the terrain and the social conditions didn't permit dogs to be kept as superfluous luxury. That doesn't mean that people did not treat their dogs with love, and the spontaneous affection of today's Westie is a sign of that. Even that has remained. The Westie as such is not an old breed, inasmuch as there were no mentions in medieval history or pictures. In Gray's "Dogs of Scotland", published in 1891, Captain Mackie describes the Westie as a "…linty white colour" and "weighing from 16 to 20 pounds". Its head was "very long", and its nose "often flesh-coloured". These dogs were also known as Poltalloch Terriers, but there were also other names: White Roseneath Terrier, Little Skye Terrier, Cairn Terrier and White Scottish Terrier. There were

various local forms, in all kinds of colours, and only in 1904 were these white dogs given the official name of West Highland White Terrier. From 1912, the Cairn Terrier was given separate championship status, and thus the official separation of the Westie and the Cairn as separate breeds became a fact. The Poltalloch Terriers were bred and kept by Colonel Malcolm, and it is thanks to him that the white colour finally determined the appearance of these lively little dogs. The events of one day decided its lot. Colonel Malcolm was out hunting when one of his favourite dogs, a small brown coarse-haired terrier, was mistaken for a rabbit and shot. Colonel Malcolm was so saddened by this event that he decided to only breed white terriers from then on, because white is a striking colour and easily distinguishes the dog from any wild animal. The White Roseneath Terriers were bred at Roseneath, the farm of the Duke of Argyll. However, there were other claims put forward for the breed. We know that Colonel Malcolm had a competitor in the shape of Dr. Flaxman. His dogs were also to be seen at shows at the time. Dr. Flaxman had a Scots Terrier bitch that gave birth to white puppies. He bred the white animals under the name Scottish White Terrier ("Dog Shows and Doggy People", 1902). With any breed, however young, there goes a certain form of

mythology. Siamese Cats are said to come from the ancient palaces of Thailand, and around the turn of the twentieth century a pair of Siamese is said to have been given to an English diplomat as a farewell gift. Some writers dispute that however and say that they were simply found 'on the street somewhere' and, because of their striking appearance (sapphire blue coat, glowing eyes and dark extremities), they were taken to England.

The Westie has a vague royal connection too. One can happily believe the story that King James I (son of Mary Queen of Scots) gave six small white terriers as a present to the King of France at the beginning of the 17th century. It's not really important whether these were Westies or one of their predecessors. One thing is certain: the Duke of Argyll's Roseneath Terrier was known prior to the 19th century as the Pure White Terrier. What is disputed is whether these white terriers were bred from light coloured Cairn Terriers or small, light Skye Terriers, or from a combination of both breeds. In view of the extremely long back that appears regularly, the Skye Terrier seems more likely to have been an ancestor than the Cairn Terrier. One who was very clear was Sir Edwin Henry Landseer who painted "Dignity and Impudence" in 1839. The lively, small dog in the right of the painting can be nothing other than a Westie. The same goes for Henry Alkens' painting "Group of Terriers" of 1820, where a predecessor of the Westie is depicted.

Breed standard

A standard has been developed for all breeds recognised by the Kennel Club for the UK (and in Europe by the F.C.I. - the umbrella organisation for Western European kennel clubs). Officially approved kennel clubs in the member countries provide a translation. This standard provides a guideline for breeders and inspectors. It is something of an ideal that dogs of the breed must strive to match. With some breeds, dogs are already bred that match the ideal. Other breeds have a long way to go. There is a list of defects for each breed. These can be serious defects that disqualify the dog, and it will be excluded from breeding. Permitted defects are not serious, but do cost points in a show.

The UK Kennel Club breed standard for the West Highland White Terrier

General Appearance
Strongly built; deep in chest and back ribs; level back and powerful quarters on muscular legs and exhibiting in a marked degree a great combination of strength and activity.

Characteristics

Small, active, game, hardy, possessed of no small amount of self-esteem with a varminty appearance.

Temperament

Alert, gay, courageous, self-reliant but friendly.

Head and Skull

Skull slightly domed; when handled across forehead presents a smooth contour. Tapering very slightly from skull at level of ears to eyes. Distance from occiput to eyes slightly greater than length of foreface. Head thickly coated with hair, and carried at right angle or less, to axis of neck. Head not to be carried in extended position. Foreface gradually tapering from eye to muzzle. Distinct stop formed by heavy, bony ridges immediately above and slightly overhanging eye, and slight indentation between eyes. Foreface not dished nor falling away quickly below eyes, where it is well made up. Jaws strong and level. Nose black and fairly large, forming smooth contour with rest of muzzle. Nose not projecting forward.

Eyes

Set wide apart, medium in size, not full, as dark as possible. Slightly sunk in head, sharp and intelligent, which, looking from under heavy eyebrows, impart a piercing look. Light coloured eyes highly undesirable.

Ears

Small, erect and carried firmly, terminating in sharp point, set neither too wide nor too close. Hair short and smooth (velvety), should not be cut. Free from any fringe at top. Round-pointed, broad, large or thick ears or too heavily coated with hair most undesirable.

Mouth

As broad between canine teeth as is consistent with varminty expression required. Teeth large for large size of dog, with regular scissor bite, i.e. upper teeth closely overlapping lower teeth and set square to the jaws.

Neck

Sufficiently long to allow proper set on of head required, muscular and gradually thickening towards base allowing neck to merge into nicely sloping shoulders.

Forequarters

Shoulders sloping backwards. Shoulder blades broad and lying close to chest wall. Shoulder joint placed forward, elbows well in, allowing foreleg to move freely, parallel to axis of body. Forelegs short and muscular, straight and thickly covered with short, hard hair.

Body

Compact. Back level, loins broad and strong. Chest deep and ribs

well arched in upper half presenting a flattish side appearance. Back ribs of considerable depth and distance from last rib of quarters as short as compatible with free movement of body.

Hindquarters
Strong, muscular and wide across top. Legs short, muscular and sinewy. Thighs very muscular and not too wide apart. Hocks bent and well set in under body so as to be fairly close to each other when standing or moving. Straight or weak hocks most undesirable.

Feet
Forefeet larger than hind, round, proportionate in size, strong, thickly padded and covered with short harsh hair. Hindfeet are smaller and thickly padded. Under surface of pads and all nails preferably black.

Tail
13-15 cms (5-6 ins) long, covered with harsh hair, no feathering, as straight as possible, carried jauntily, not gay or carried over back. A long tail undesirable, and on no account should tails be docked.

Gait/Movement
Free, straight and easy all round. In front, legs freely extended forward from shoulder. Hind movement free, strong and close. Stifle and hocks well flexed and hocks drawn under body giving drive.

Stiff, stilted movement behind and cowhocks highly undesirable.

Coat
Double coated. Outer coat consists of harsh hair, about 5 cms (2 ins) long, free from any curl. Undercoat, which resembles fur, short, soft and close. Open coats most undesirable.

Colour
White.

Size
Height at withers approximately 28 cms (11 ins).

Faults
Any departure from the foregoing points should be considered a fault and the seriousness with which the fault should be regarded should be in exact proportion to its degree.

Note
Male animals should have two apparently normal testicles fully descended into the scrotum.

September 2000

Reproduced by courtesy of the Kennel Club of Great Britain

Buying a Westie

Once you've made that properly considered decision to buy a dog, there are several options. Should it be a puppy, an adult dog, or even an older dog?

Should it be a bitch or dog, a pedigree dog or a cross? Of course, the question also comes up as to where to buy your dog - from a private person, a reliable breeder or an animal shelter? For you and the animal, it's vital to get these questions sorted out in advance. You want a dog that will fit your circumstances properly. With a puppy, you get a playful energetic housemate that will easily adapt to a new environment. If you want something quieter, an older dog is a good choice.

Pros and cons of the West Highland White Terrier
Westies were originally bred for (underground) hunting of foxes, otters, badgers, rats etc. They needed courage, resolution, strength and perseverance.

The Westie still possesses these characteristics today. Some people forget that however. The Westie is often perceived as a sweet little lap dog, but that is something it most certainly is not. This term generally will not apply to a Westie. As cute as they may look with their round white head, they are and remain a real terrier. You will need to give your Westie a rigorous upbringing. Yes is yes, and no is no. That doesn't mean it needs a harsh and strict approach (although some dogs do need that), but it must know from the very beginning that you're the boss.
Attending a puppy training or obedience course is certainly to be recommended, and if you're as persevering as your Westie, you'll get on fine.

Male or female?

Whether you choose a male or a female puppy, or an adult dog or bitch, is an entirely personal decision. A male typically needs more leadership because he tends to be more dominant by nature. He will try to play boss over other dogs and, if he gets the chance, over people too. In the wild, the most dominant dog (or wolf) is always the leader of the pack. In many cases this is a male. A bitch is much more focussed on her master, she sees him as the pack leader.

A puppy test is good for defining the kind of character a young dog will develop. During a test one usually sees that a dog is more dominant than a bitch. You can often quickly recognise the bossy, the adventurous and the cautious characters. So visit the litter a couple of times early on. Try to pick a puppy that suits your own personality. A dominant dog, for instance, needs a strong hand. It will often try to see just how far it can go. You must regularly make it clear who's the boss, and that it must obey all the members of the family.

When bitches are sexually mature, they will go into season. On average, a bitch is in season twice a year for about two or three weeks. This is the fertile period when she can be mated. Particularly in the second half of her season, she will want to go looking for a dog to mate with, and she can also become pregnant. A male dog will show more masculine traits once he is sexually mature. He will make sure other dogs know what territory is his by urinating as often as possible in as many places as he can. He is also difficult to restrain if there's a bitch in season nearby. As far as normal care is concerned there is little difference between a dog and a bitch.

Puppy or adult?

After you've made the decision for a male or female, the next question comes up. Should it be a puppy or an adult dog? Your household circumstances usually play a major role here.

Of course, it's great having a sweet little puppy in the house, but bringing up a young dog requires a lot of time. In the first year of its life it learns more than during the rest of its life. This is the period when the foundations are laid for elementary matters such as house-training, obedience and social behaviour. You must reckon with the fact that your puppy will keep you busy for a couple of hours a day, certainly in the first few months. You won't need so much time with a grown dog. It has already been brought up (but this doesn't mean it won't need correcting from time to time!).

A puppy will no doubt leave a trail of destruction in its wake for the first few months. With a little bad luck, this will cost you a number of rolls of wallpaper, some good shoes and a few socks. In the worst case you'll be left with some chewed furniture. Some puppies even manage to tear curtains from their rails. With good upbringing this 'vandalism' will quickly disappear, but you won't have to worry about this if you get an older dog.

The greatest advantage of a puppy, of course, is that you can bring it up your own way. And the upbringing a dog gets (or doesn't get) is a major influence on its whole character. Finally, financial aspects may play a role in your choice. A puppy is generally (much) more expensive than an adult dog, not only in purchase price but also in 'maintenance'. A puppy needs to go to the vet's more often for the necessary vaccinations and check-ups.

Overall, bringing up a puppy involves a good deal of energy, time and money, but you have its upbringing in your own hands. An adult dog costs less money and time, but its character is already formed. You should also try to find out about the background of an adult dog. Its previous owner may have formed its character in somewhat less positive ways.

Two dogs?

Having two or more dogs in the house is not just nice for us, but also for the animals themselves. Dogs get a lot of pleasure from their own company. After all, they are pack animals. If you're sure that you want two young dogs, it's best not to buy them at the same time. Bringing a dog up and establishing the bond between dog and master takes time, and you need to give a lot of attention to your dog in this phase. Having two puppies in the house means you have to divide your attention between them. Apart from that, there's a danger that they will focus on one another rather than on their master. Buy the second pup when the first is (almost) an adult.

Two adult dogs can happily be brought into the home together. Getting a puppy when the first dog is somewhat older often has a positive effect on the older dog. The influence of the puppy almost seems to give it a second childhood. The older dog, if it's been well brought up, can help with the upbringing of the puppy. Young dogs like to imitate the behaviour of their elders. Don't forget to give both dogs the same amount of attention. Take the puppy out alone at least once per day during the first eighteen months. Give the older dog enough opportunity to get some peace and quiet. It won't want an enthusiastic youngster running around under its feet all the time.

The combination of a male and female needs special attention. If you don't want puppies from your dogs (i.e. never, definitely), you must take measures to stop this happening. Besides sterilising the female, castrating the male is also an option. However, the latter is usually only done on medical advice or to correct behaviour problems.

A dog and children

Dogs and children are a great combination. They can play together and get great pleasure out of each other's company. Moreover, children need to learn how to handle living beings; they develop respect and a sense of responsibility by caring for a dog (or other pets). However sweet a dog is, children must understand that it is an animal and not a toy. A dog isn't comfortable when it's being messed around with. It can become frightened, timid and even aggressive. So make it clear what a dog likes and what it doesn't. Look for ways the child can play with the dog, perhaps a game of hide and seek where the child hides and the dog has to find it. Even a simple tennis ball can give enormous pleasure. Children must learn to leave a dog in peace when it doesn't want to play any more.

The dog must also have its own place where it's not disturbed. Have children help with your dog's care as much as possible. A strong bond will be the result.

The arrival of a baby also means changes in the life of a dog. Before the birth you can help get the dog acquainted with the new situation. Let it sniff at the new things in the house and it will quickly accept them. When the baby has arrived, involve the dog as much as possible in day-by-day events, but make sure it gets plenty of attention too. NEVER leave a dog alone with young children. Crawling infants sometimes make unexpected movements, which can easily frighten a dog. And infants are hugely curious, and may try to find out whether the tail is really fastened to the dog, or whether its eyes come out, just like they do with their cuddly toys. But a dog is a dog and it will defend itself when it feels threatened.

Where to buy

There are various ways of acquiring a dog. The decision for a puppy or an adult dog will also define for the most part where to buy your dog. If it's to be a puppy, then you need to find a breeder with a litter. If you chose a popular breed,

like the Westie, there is choice enough. But you may also face the problem that there are so many puppies on sale that have only been bred for profit's sake. You can see how many puppies are for sale by looking in the regional newspaper every Saturday. Some of these dogs have a pedigree, but many don't. These breeders often don't watch out for breed-specific illnesses and any hereditary breeding faults and defects; puppies are separated from their mother as fast as possible and are thus insufficiently socialised. Never buy a puppy that is too young, or whose mother you weren't able to see. Fortunately there are also enough bona-fide breeders of West Highland White Terriers. Try to visit a number of breeders before you actually buy your puppy. Ask if the breeder is prepared to help you after you've bought your puppy, and to help you find solutions for any problems that may come up.

To put aspiring puppy owners into contact with a breeder that breeds according to the breed association standards, many kennel clubs offer

Things to watch out for

Buying a puppy is no simple matter. You must pay attention to the following:

- Never buy a puppy on impulse, even if it is love at first sight. A dog is a living being that will need care and attention over a long period. It is not a toy that you can put away when you've finished with it.

a puppy information service. Finally, you should be aware that pedigree certificates are also issued for the offspring of animals with hereditary defects, or those that have not been examined for these. A pedigree says nothing about the health of the animals bred. If you're looking for an adult dog, it's best to contact the breed association, who often help place adult dogs that can no longer be kept by their owners because of personal circumstances (impulse buying, moving home, divorce etc.).

- Take a good look at the mother. Is she calm, nervous, aggressive, well cared-for or neglected? The behaviour and condition of the mother is not only a sign of the quality of the breeder, but also of the puppy you're about to buy.
- Avoid buying a puppy whose mother has been kept only in a kennel. A young dog needs as many different impressions as possible in its first few months, including living in a family group. It gets used to people and possibly other pets. Kennel dogs miss these experiences and are inadequately socialised.
- Always ask to see the parents' papers (vaccination certificates, pedigrees, official reports on health examinations).
- Never buy a puppy younger than eight weeks.
- Put all agreements with the breeder in writing. A model agreement is available from the breed association.

Travelling with your Westie

There are a few things to think about before travelling with your dog. While one dog may enjoy travelling, another may hate it. You may like holidays in far-away places, but it's questionable whether your dog will agree with you.

That very first trip

The first trip of a puppy's life is also the most nerve-wrecking. This is the trip from the breeder's to its new home. Try to pick your puppy up early in the morning. It then has plenty of time to get used to its new situation. Ask the breeder not to feed it that day. The young animal will be overwhelmed by all kinds of new experiences. Firstly, it's away from its mother; it's in a small room (the car) with all its different smells, noises and strange people. So there's a big chance that the puppy will be car-sick this first time, with the annoying consequence that it will remember travelling in the car as an unpleasant experience. So it's important to make this first trip as pleasant as possible. When picking up a puppy, always take someone with you who can sit in the back seat with the puppy on his or her lap and talk to it calmly. If it's too warm for the puppy, a place on the floor at the feet of your companion is ideal. The pup will lie there relatively quietly and may even take a nap. Ask the breeder for a cloth or something else from the puppies' basket or bed that carries a familiar scent. The puppy can lie on this in the car, and it will also help if it feels alone during the first nights at home.

If the trip home is a long one, then stop for a break (once in a while). Let your puppy roam and sniff around (on the lead!), offer it a little drink and, if necessary, let it do its business. Do take care to lay an old towel in the car. It can happen that the puppy, in its ner-

vousness, may urinate or be sick. It's also good advice to give a puppy positive experiences with car journeys. Make short trips to nice places where you can walk and play with it. A dog that doesn't like travelling in a car can cause a lot of problems.

Taking your Westie on holiday

When making holiday plans, you also need to think about what you're going to do with your dog during that time. Are you taking it with you, putting it into kennels or leaving it with friends? In any event there are a number of things you need to do in good time. If you want to take your dog with you, you need to be sure in good time that it will be welcome at your holiday home, and what rules there are. If you're going abroad it will need certain vaccinations and a health certificate, which normally need to be done four weeks before departure.

You must also be sure that you've made all the arrangements necessary to bring your dog back home to the UK, without it needing to go into quarantine under the rabies regulations. Your vet can give you the most recent information.

If your trip is to southern Europe, ask for a treatment against tics (you can read more about this in the chapter on parasites).

Although dog-owners usually enjoy taking their dog on holiday, you must seriously ask yourself whether the dog feels that way too. Dogs certainly don't always feel comfortable in a hot country. Days spent travelling in a car are also often not their preference, and some dogs suffer badly from car-sickness. There are good

medicines for this, but it's questionable whether you're doing your dog a favour with them. If you do decide to take it with you, make regular stops at safe places during your journey, so that your dog can have a good run. Take plenty of fresh drinking water with you, as well as the food your dog is used to. Don't leave your dog in the car that is parked in the sun. It can quickly be overcome by the heat, with even fatal consequences. If you can't avoid it, park the car in the shade if at all possible, and leave a window open for a little fresh air. Even if you've taken these precautions, never stay away long!

If you're travelling by plane or ship, make sure in good time that your dog can travel with you and what rules you need to observe. You will need some time to make all the arrangements. Maybe you decide not to take your dog with you, and you then need to find somewhere for it to stay. Arrangements for a place in kennels need to be made well in advance, and there may be certain vaccinations required, which need to be given a minimum of one month before the stay.

If your dog can't be accommodated in the homes of relatives or friends, it might be possible to have an acquaintance stay in your house. This also needs to be arranged well in advance, as it may be difficult to find someone who can do this.

Always ensure that your dog can be traced should it run away or get lost while on holiday. A little tube with your address or a tag with home and holiday address can prevent a lot of problems.

Moving home

Dogs generally become more attached to humans than to the house they live in. Moving home is usually not a problem for them. But it can be useful before moving to let the dog get to know its new home and the area around it.

If you can, leave your dog with relatives or friends (or in kennels) on the day of the move. The chance of it running away or getting lost is then practically nonexistent. When your move is complete, you can pick up your dog and let it quietly get familiar with its new home and environment. Give it its own place in the house at once and it will quickly adapt. During the first week or so, always walk your dog on a lead because an animal can also get lost in new surroundings. Always take a different route so it quickly gets to know the neighbourhood.

Don't forget to get your new address and phone number engraved on the dog's tag. Send a change of address notice to the chip or tattoo registration office. Dogs must sometimes be registered in a new community.

Feeding your Westie

A dog will actually eat a lot more than just meat. In the wild it would eat its prey complete with skin and fur, including the bones, stomach, and the innards with their semi digested vegetable material.

In this way the dog supplements its meat menu with the vitamins and minerals it needs. This is also the basis for feeding a domestic dog.

Ready-made foods

It's not easy for a layman to put together a complete menu for a dog that includes all the necessary proteins, fats, vitamins and minerals in just the right proportions and quantities. Meat alone is certainly not a complete meal for a dog. It contains too little calcium. A calcium deficiency over time will lead to bone defects, and for a fast-growing puppy this can lead to serious skeletal deformities.

If you put its food together yourself, you can easily give your dog too much in terms of vitamins and minerals, which can also be bad for your dog's health. You can avoid these problems by giving it ready-made food of a good brand. These products are well-balanced and contain everything your dog needs. Supplements such as vitamin preparations are superfluous. The amount of food your dog needs depends on its weight and activity level. You can find guidelines on the packaging. Split the food into two meals per day if possible, and always ensure there's a bowl of fresh drinking water next to its food.

Give your dog the time to digest its food and don't let it outside straight after a meal. A dog should also never play on a full stomach. This can cause stomach torsion, (the stomach turning over), which can be fatal for your dog.

Because the nutritional needs of a dog vary, among other things, on its age and way of life, there are many different types of dog food available. There are "light" foods for less active dogs, "energy" foods for working dogs and "senior" foods for the older dog.

Puppy chunks

There is now a wide assortment of puppy chunks on the market. These chunks contain a higher content of growth-promoting nutrients, such as protein and calcium. Give your puppy only special puppy chunks such as Royal Canin Size, Hill's Canine, Eukanuba or Advance Junior.

Canned foods, mixer and dry foods

Ready-made foods available at pet shops or in the supermarket can roughly be split into canned food, mixer and dry food. Whichever form you choose, ensure that it's a complete food with all the necessary ingredients. You can see this on the packaging.

Most dogs love canned food. Although the better brands are composed well, they do have one disadvantage: they are soft. A dog fed only on canned food will sooner or later have problems with its teeth (plaque, paradontosis). Besides canned food, give your dog hard foods at certain times or a dog chew, such as Nylabone.

Mixer is a food consisting of chunks, dried vegetables and grains. Almost all moisture has been extracted. The advantages of mixer are that it is light and keeps well. You add a certain amount of water and the meal is ready. A disadvantage is that it must definitely not be fed without water. Without the extra fluid, mixer will absorb the fluids present in the stomach, with serious results. Should your dog manage to get at the bag and enjoy its contents, you must immediately give it plenty to drink.

Dry chunks have also had the moisture extracted but not as much as mixer. The advantage of dry foods is that they are hard, forcing the dog to use its jaws, removing plaque and massaging the gums.

Dog chew products

Of course, once in a while you want to spoil your dog with something extra. Don't give it pieces of cheese or sausage as these contain too much salt and fat. There are various products available that a dog will find delicious and which are also healthy, especially for its teeth. You'll find a large range of varying quality in the pet shop.

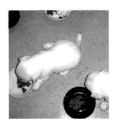

The butcher's left-overs

The bones of slaughtered animals have traditionally been given to the dog, and dogs love them, but they are not without risks. Pork and poultry bones are too weak. They can splinter and cause serious injury to the intestines. Beef bones are more suitable, but they must first be cooked to kill off dangerous bacteria. Pet shops carry a range of smoked, cooked and dried abattoir residue, such as pigs' ears, bull penis, tripe sticks, oxtails, gullet, dried muscle meat, and hoof chews.

Fresh meat

If you do want to give your dog fresh meat occasionally, never give it raw, but always boiled or roasted. Raw (or not fully cooked) pork or chicken can contain life-threatening bacteria. Chicken can be contaminated by the notorious salmonella bacteria, while pork can carry the Aujeszky virus. This disease is incurable and

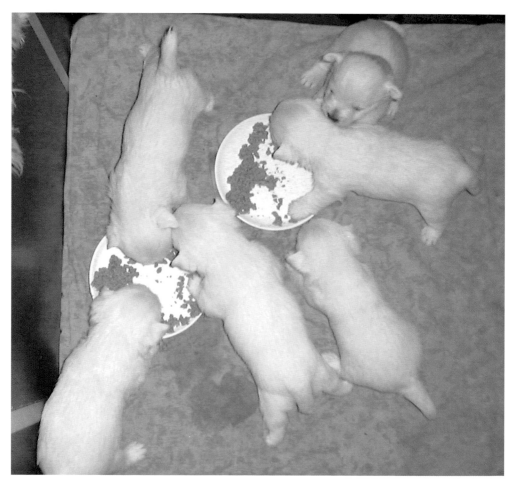

will quickly lead to the death of your pet.

Buffalo or cowhide chews

Dog chews are mostly made of beef or buffalo hide. Chews are usually knotted or pressed hide and can come in the form of little shoes, twisted sticks, lollies, balls and various other shapes; nice to look at and a nice change.

Warning: Some dogs are so crazy about buffalo hide that they become really greedy and piggish with them. This can cause them to swallow them by accident with suffocation being a possible result.

Munchy sticks

Munchy sticks are green, yellow, red or brown coloured sticks of various thicknesses. They consist of ground buffalo hide with a number of often undefined additives. The composition and quality of these between-meal treats is not always clear. Some are fine, but there have also been sticks found to contain high levels of cardboard and even paint residues. Choose a product whose ingredients are clearly described.

Overweight?

Recent investigations have shown that many dogs are overweight. A dog usually gets too fat because of over-feeding and lack of exercise. Use of medicines or a disease is rarely the cause. Dogs that get too

fat are often given too much food or treats between meals. Gluttony or boredom can also be a cause, and a dog often puts on weight following castration or sterilisation. Due to changes in hormone levels, it becomes less active and consumes less energy. Finally, simply too little exercise alone can lead to a dog becoming overweight.

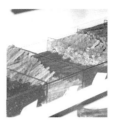

You can use the following rule of thumb to check whether your dog is overweight: you should be able to feel its ribs, but not see them. If you can't feel its ribs then your dog is much too fat. Overweight dogs live a passive life, they play too little and tire quickly. They also suffer from all kinds of medical problems (problems in joints and heart conditions). They usually die younger too.

So it's important to make sure your dog doesn't get too fat. Always follow the guidelines on food packaging. Adapt them if your dog is less active or gets lots of snacks. Try to make sure your dog gets plenty of exercise by playing and running with it as much as you can. If your dog starts to show signs of putting on weight you can switch to a low-calorie food. If it's really too fat and reducing its food quantity doesn't help, then a special diet is the only solution.

Caring for your Westie

Proper (daily) care is of great importance for your dog. A well cared-for dog runs much less risk of becoming ill. Caring for your dog is not only necessary, but also fun. Master and dog spend some time together and it's an excellent time for a game and a cuddle.

Grooming

Over the years the West Highland White Terrier has changed a lot in appearance. If we look at photos dating back eighty years or so and compare them with today's animals, we can see some differences. The West Highland White Terrier has changed from a simple white working terrier with very short bristle hair to the 'chocolate box' image with lots of superfluous fur as we know it today, but still with the same character.

The coat of today's West Highland White Terrier needs a lot more maintenance, especially as very few Westies still do the same job and lose their dead hair in bushes and burrows. Our expectations of the dog's appearance have also changed; these days, a dog should always look well groomed and smell fresh.

Brushing and Combing

The most important part of coat care as far as the owner is concerned is daily brushing and combing. That this is more difficult for some people than you might think is proven by the Westies that show up at dog beauty parlours. It is vital to get a puppy used to this ritual from the very beginning and to brush and comb it daily, preferably on a table. "Teach 'em young" applies here too.

First work through the coat with a very coarse comb. The best result is achieved by starting underneath and combing the fur in layers, working away from the skin. The inside of its legs, breech and belly must not be forgotten. Then the dog is brushed into 'shape' using a shaped brush.

By brushing and combing daily, it should rarely or never be necessary to bathe a West Highland White Terrier, but if this does become necessary (Westies enjoy a roll in something that 'smells nice' too), then use a special dog shampoo. The acidity level of a dog's skin is much different to that of a human and dog shampoos are specially developed for it.

Weekly inspection

However, the West Highland White Terrier consists of more than just fur, and its eyes, ears, teeth, nails, soles of the feet and the genital areas also need care. Because of their copious fur, any problems here might not be as easy to spot as on short-haired dogs.

Ears: The ear channel should be pink in colour and smell fresh. Pluck out any hair growth, otherwise dirt and ear wax can build up in it, leading to an infection.

Eyes: The 'sleepies' in the corner of your Westie's eyes are black and dry. Wipe them away gently using a clean finger nail every day and your dog's face will be 'awake' again.

If these grains are allowed to stay in the eye too long, the skin below may become infected. If the discharge is moist or pussy, contact your vet. It might be a sign of an infection of the eye or the tear ducts.

Teeth: The gums should be pink (on very strongly pigmented West Highland White Terriers, they may be black) and the teeth bright white. By letting your Westie use its teeth by giving it hard chunks or dog chews, such as Nylabone, you are helping to keep its teeth in good condition. Regular cleaning also promotes blood flow in the gums, preventing inflammation. Any plaque should be removed by a vet or dog beauty parlour. With a young dog, it's important to make sure its milk teeth give way to its adult teeth in time. Double teeth can seriously impair the alignment of its teeth.

Nails: A West Highland White Terrier that meets the requirements of the breed standard has black toe nails. Fortunately for those who have to clip its nails, almost every Westie has one or more of lighter colour. This makes the 'quick' easier to see. Never clip into the quick because this will cause heavy bleeding and the quick may need to be cauterised. If the dog stands correctly, its nails will wear themselves down naturally. Otherwise they must be regularly clipped or filed back. Little thumbs and any dew claws

(toes and nails that sit higher on the foot) must also be regularly kept in shape because these don't touch the ground and thus don't get worn down.

Foot-soles: Hair also grows between the cushions on the underside of the feet. If this is allowed to get too long, tangles can result which makes walking difficult for your dog. It feels something like you having a stone in your shoe. This hair needs to clipped away with great care, as the skin here is very thin and soft. The fur on the feet should be kept short in the winter too, otherwise lumps of ice can form when it's been snowing.

Genital areas: The anal and genital area is often 'forgotten' by many people. Why? Perhaps they feel a little embarrassed at touching their dog's genitals? However, the West Highland White Terrier will feel a lot better if this area is properly looked after. Of course, the anus must be kept free of any remains of droppings. Westies with normal bowel movements don't have problems in this respect, but if your dog has diarrhoea, then its anal area must be thoroughly washed and then brushed through.

Every (uncastrated) male has problems with foreskin infections to a greater or lesser extent. This is not so serious as long as it's not a problem for its owner, but it is a

good idea to keep the fur around its penis short to prevent sticky clumps and smells developing. For those who find this foreskin infection unpleasant, a good foreskin cleaner used regularly will keep this problem under control.

Young bitches can often have problems with vaginitis before their first season. This is a slight infection of the vagina with a little sticky discharge. The vagina must be kept clean by washing and by keeping the fur short until their first season. The vagina needs special attention during the bitch's season with careful washing and brushing. The animal will lick herself regularly during this period and this, together with the discharge, can easily cause small clumps.

If a West Highland White Terrier is regularly groomed in specialist animal beauty parlours, the above will all be taken care of professionally.

Plucking

Every West Highland White Terrier CAN AND MUST BE PLUCKED.

Plucking involves pulling dead hair, with its roots, out of the skin. If this is not done, the coat will 'suffocate' because there is too little or no space for healthy new hair to grow.

If plucking is done properly by an expert, it won't hurt the dog and, at the same time, the coat is kept in form and at the right length. In principle, the coat is ready for a trim twice a year. At that time, the whole outer coat can be plucked out, and the dog is now 'dressed' in its undercoat. If the undercoat is very thin or not present at all, the result may appear a little 'pig-like' and the transition to those parts with longer fur will be unattractive. It's therefore a good idea to have a West Highland White Terrier plucked at least four times a year. In this way, half the coat is removed each time and a firm new layer will have developed beneath it. The West Highland White Terrier now meets the requirements of the breed standard with a nice tight coat.

Soft coats: Unfortunately, there are more and more West Highland White Terriers that no longer have a really firm coat, but soft curly hair. Their fully covered faces look very pretty, but these types of coat demand a lot more mainte-nance by owner and beautician. Four trimming sessions per year are not enough for these dogs and they frequently need restyling six times a year. Brushing this soft fur is also more difficult as it tangles more easily.

Styling

Regular plucking of the West Highland White Terrier is not just good for healthy growth of its new coat. The style the dog is trimmed in is also important. To keep a Westie in the right form needs a certain knowledge of the breed standard. This includes all the points that need to be observed.

For example: The West Highland White Terrier should have a small pointed ear. If the fur around the ear is trimmed too short, a 'Dumbo' effect can quickly appear. Trimming done wrongly can ruin your Westie's appearance. It can take a whole year to get a poorly trimmed Westie back into shape. To avoid this, make sure you find a good address to have your Westie plucked. In the last few years, a number of West Highland Terrier Specialists have been available who will guarantee to give your dog back to you in the style the standard calls for. The breed association can provide you with addresses for such specialists.

Bringing up your Westie

It is very important that your dog is properly brought up and obedient. Not only will this bring you more pleasure, but it's also nicer for your environment.

A puppy can learn what it may and may not do by playing. Rewards and consistency are important tools in bringing up a dog. Reward it with your voice, a stroke or something tasty and it will quickly learn to obey. A puppy training course can also help you along the way.

(Dis)obedience

A dog that won't obey you is not just a problem for you, but also for your surroundings. It's therefore important to avoid unwanted behaviour. In fact, this is what training your dog is all about, so get started early. 'Start 'em young!' applies to dogs too. An untrained dog is not just a nuisance, but can also cause dangerous situations, running into the road, chasing joggers or jumping at

people. A dog must be trained out of this undesirable behaviour as quickly as possible. The longer you let it go on, the more difficult it will become to correct. The best thing to do is to attend a special obedience course. This won't only help to correct the dog's behaviour, but its owner also learns how to handle undesirable behaviour at home. A dog must not only obey its master during training, but at home too.

Always be consistent when training good behaviour and correcting annoying behaviour. This means a dog may always behave in a certain way, or must never behave that way. Reward it for good behaviour and never punish it after the fact for any wrong-doing. If your dog finally comes to you after you've been calling it a long time, then reward it. If you're angry because you had to wait so long, it may feel it's actually being punished for coming. It will probably not obey at all the next time for fear of punishment.

Try to take no notice of undesirable behaviour. Your dog will perceive your reaction (even a negative one) as a reward for this behaviour. If you need to correct the dog, then do this immediately. Use your voice or grip it by the scruff of its neck and push it to the ground. This is the way a mother dog calls her pups to order. Rewards for good behaviour are, by far, preferable to punishment; they always get a better result.

House-training

The very first training (and one of the most important) that a dog needs is house-training. The basis for good house-training is keeping a good eye on your puppy. If you pay attention, you will notice that it will sniff a long time and turn around a certain spot before doing its business there. Pick it up gently and place it outside, always at the same place. Reward it abundantly if it does its business there.

Another good moment for house-training is after eating or sleeping. A puppy often needs to do its business at these times. Let it relieve itself before playing with it, other-

wise it will forget to do so and you'll not reach your goal. For the first few days, take your puppy out for a walk just after it's eaten or woken up. It will quickly learn the meaning, especially if it's rewarded with a dog biscuit for a successful attempt. Of course, it's not always possible to go out after every snack or snooze. Lay newspapers at different spots in the house. Whenever the pup needs to do its business, place it on a newspaper. After some time it will start to look for a place itself. Then start to reduce the number of newspapers until there is just one left, at the front or back door. The puppy will learn to go to the door if it needs to relieve itself. Then you put it on the lead and go out with it. Finally you can remove the last newspaper. Your puppy is now house-trained.

One thing that certainly won't work is punishing an accident after the fact. A dog whose nose is rubbed in its urine or its droppings won't understand that at all. It will only get frightened of you. Rewarding works much better than punishment. An indoor kennel or cage can be a good tool in helping with house-training. A puppy won't foul its own nest, so a kennel can be a good solution for the night, or during periods in the day when you can't watch it. But a kennel must not become a prison where your dog is locked up day and night.

Basic obedience

The basic commands for an obedient dog are those for sit, lie down, come and stay. But a puppy should first learn its name. Use it as much as possible from the first day on followed by a friendly 'Come!'. Reward it with your voice and a stroke when it comes to you. Your puppy will quickly recognise the intention and has now learned its first command in a playful manner. Don't be too harsh with a young puppy, and don't always punish it immediately if it doesn't always react in the right way. When you call your puppy to you in this way have it come right to you. You can teach a

pup to sit by holding a piece of dog biscuit above its nose and then slowly moving it backwards. The puppy's head will also move backwards until its hind legs slowly go down. At that moment you call 'Sit!'. After a few attempts, it will quickly know this nice game. Use the 'Sit!' command before giving your dog its food, putting it on the lead, or before it's allowed to cross the road.

Teaching the command to lie down is similar. Instead of moving the piece of dog biscuit backwards, move it down vertically until your hand reaches the ground and then forwards. The

dog will also move its forepaws forwards and lie down on its own. At that moment call 'Lie down!' or 'Lay!'. This command is useful when you want a dog to be quiet.

Two people are needed for the 'Come!' command. One holds the dog back while the other runs away. After about fifteen metres, he stops and enthusiastically calls 'Come!'. The other person now lets the dog go, and it should obey the command at once. Again you reward it abundantly. The 'Come!' command is useful in many situations and good for safety too.

A dog learns to stay from the sitting or lying position. While it's sitting or lying down, you call the command 'Stay!' and then step back one step. If the dog moves with you, quietly put it back in position, without displaying anger. If you do react angrily, you're actually punishing it for coming to you, and you'll only confuse your dog. It can't understand that coming is rewarded one time, and punished another. Once the dog stays nicely reward it abundantly. Practise this exercise with increasing distances (at first no more than one metre). The 'Stay!' command is useful when getting out of the car.

Courses

Obedience courses to help you bring up your dog are available across the country. These courses are not just informative, but also fun for dog and master.

With a puppy, you can begin with a puppy course. This is designed to provide the basic training. A puppy that has attended such a course has learned about all kinds of things that will confront it in later life: other dogs, humans, traffic and what these mean. The puppy will also learn obedience and to follow a number of basic commands. Apart from all that, attention will be given to important subjects such as brushing, being alone, travelling in a car, and doing its business in the right places.

The next step after a puppy course is a course for young dogs. This course repeats the basic exercises and ensures that the growing dog doesn't get into bad habits. After this, the dog can move on to an

obedience course for full-grown dogs. For more information on where to find courses in your area, contact your local kennel club. You can get its address from the Kennel Club of Great Britain in London. In some areas, the RSPCA organises obedience classes and your local branch may be able to give you information.

Play and toys
There are various ways to play with your dog, You can romp and run with it, but also play a number of games, such as retrieving, tug-of-war, hide-and-seek and catch. A tennis ball is ideal for retrieving, you can play tug-of-war with an old sock or a special tugging rope. Start with tug-of-war only when your dog is a year old. A puppy must first get its second teeth and then they need several months to strengthen. There's a real chance of your dog's teeth becoming deformed if you start too young. You can use almost anything for a game of hide-and-seek. A frisbee is ideal for catching games. Never use too small a ball for games. It can easily get lodged into the dog's throat.

Play is extremely important. Not only does it strengthen the bond between dog and master, but it's also healthy for both. Make sure that you're the one that ends the game. Only stop when the dog has brought back the ball or frisbee, and make sure you always win the tug-of-war. This confirms your dominant position in the hierarchy. Use these toys only during play so that the dog doesn't forget their significance. When choosing a special dog toy, remember that dogs are hardly careful with them. So always buy toys of good quality that a dog can't easily destroy.

Be very careful with sticks and twigs. The latter, particularly, can easily splinter. A splinter of wood in your dog's throat or intestines can cause awful problems. Throwing sticks or twigs can also be dangerous. If they stick into the ground a dog can easily run into them with an open mouth.

If you would like to do more than just play games, you can now also play sports with your dog. For people who want to do more, there are various other sporting alternatives such as flyball, agility, and obedience.

The Terrier temperament

West Highland White Terriers are practically never aggressive, but by nature have a snappy character as is the case for most terrier types. That means they are less tolerant towards other males and need a very rigorous upbringing and training.

Fear

The source of anxious behaviour can often be traced to the first weeks of a dog's life. A shortage of new experiences during this important phase (also called the 'socialisation phase') has great influence on its later behaviour. A dog that never encountered humans, other dogs or animals during the socialisation phase will be afraid of them later. This fear is common in dogs brought up in a barn or kennel, with almost no contact with humans. As we saw, fear can lead to aggressive behaviour, so it's important that a puppy gets as many new impressions as possible in the first weeks of its life. Take it with you into town in the car or on the bus, walk it down busy streets and allow it to have plenty of contact with people, other dogs and other animals.

It's a huge task to turn an anxious, poorly socialised dog into a real pet. It will probably take an enormous amount of attention, love, patience and energy to get such an animal used to everything around it. Reward it often and give it plenty of time to adapt and, over time, it will learn to trust you and become less anxious. Try not to force anything, because that will always have the reverse effect. Here too, an obedience course can help a lot. A dog can be especially afraid of strangers. Have visitors give it something tasty as a treat. Put a can of dog biscuits by the door so that your visitors can spoil your dog when they arrive. Here again, don't try to force anything. If the dog is still frightened, leave it in peace.

Dogs are often frightened in certain situations; well-known examples are thunderstorms and fireworks. In these cases try to ignore their anxious behaviour. If you react to their whimpering and

whining, it's the same as rewarding it. If you ignore its fear completely, the dog will quickly learn that nothing is wrong. You can speed up this 'learning process' by rewarding its positive behaviour.

Rewarding

Rewarding forms the basis for bringing up a dog. Rewarding good behaviour works far better than punishing bad behaviour and rewarding is also much more fun. Recently, the opinions on upbringing for dogs have gradually changed. In the past the proper way to correct bad behaviour was regarded as a sharp pull on the lead. Today, experts view rewards as a positive incentive to get dogs to do what we expect of them. There are many ways to reward a dog. The usual ways are a stroke or a friendly word, even without a tasty treat to go with it. Of course, a piece of dog biscuit does wonders when you're training a puppy. Be sure you always have something delicious in your pocket to reward good behaviour. Another form of reward is play. Whenever a dog notices you have a ball in your pocket, it won't go far from your side. As soon as you've finished playing, put the ball away. This way your dog will always do its best in exchange for a game.

Despite the emphasis you put on rewarding good behaviour, a dog can sometimes be a nuisance or disobedient. You must correct such behaviour immediately. Always be consistent: 'no' must always be 'no'.

Barking

Dogs that bark too much and too often are a nuisance for their surroundings. A dog-owner may tolerate barking up to a point, but neighbours are often annoyed by the unnecessary noise. Don't encourage your puppy to bark and yelp. Of course, it should be able to announce its presence, but if it goes on barking it must be called to order with a strict 'Quiet!'. If a puppy fails to obey, just hold its muzzle closed with your hand.

A dog will sometimes bark for long periods when left alone. It feels threatened and tries to get someone's attention by barking. There are special training programmes for this problem, where dogs learn that being alone is nothing to be afraid of, and that its

master will always return. You can practise this with your dog at home. Leave the room and come back in at once. Reward your dog if it stays quiet. Gradually increase the length of your absences and keep rewarding it as long as it remains quiet. Never punish the dog if it does bark or yelp. It will never understand punishment afterwards, and this will only make the problem worse. Never go back into the room as long as your dog is barking, as it will view this as a reward. You might want to make the dog feel more comfortable by switching the radio on for company during your absence. It will eventually learn that you always come back and the barking will reduce. If you don't get the required result, attend an obedience course.

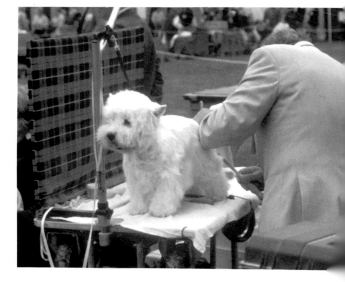

Breeding

Dogs, and thus also the West Highland Whiter Terrier, follow their instincts, and reproduction is one of nature's important processes.

For people who enjoy breeding dogs this is a positive circumstance. Those who simply want a' cosy companion' however, do not need the regular adventures with females on heat and unrestrainable males. Knowing a little about breeding in dogs will help you to understand why they behave the way they do, and the measures you need to take when this happens.

Liability
Breeding dogs is not just simply 1+1= many. If you're planning to breed with your Westie, be on your guard, otherwise the whole affair can turn into a financial drama because, under the law, a breeder is liable for the 'quality' of his puppies.

The breed clubs place strict conditions on animals used for breeding. (See the chapter Your Westie's health). If you do plan to breed a litter of puppies but don't have enough knowledge, the breed association can give good advice. Be careful because, if your puppies later show symptoms of hereditary defects, you can be held liable by the new owners for any costs arising from them. These (veterinary) costs can be enormous! So contact the breeder of your female or the breed association if you plan to breed a litter of West Highland White Terriers.

The female in season
Bitches become sexually mature at about six to nine months. Then they go into season for the first

time. They are 'on heat' for two to three weeks. During this period they discharge little drops of blood and they are very attractive to males. The bitch is fertile during the second half of her season, and will accept a male to mate. The best time for mating is then between the ninth and thirteenth day of her season. A female's first season is often shorter and less severe than those that follow. If you do want to breed with your female you must allow this first and the second season to pass. Most bitches go into season twice per year. If you do plan to breed with your Westie in the future, then sterilisation is not an option to prevent unwanted off-spring. A temporary solution is a contraceptive injection, although this is controversial because of side effects such as womb infections.

Phantom pregnancy

A phantom pregnancy is a not uncommon occurrence. The female behaves as if she has a litter. She takes all kinds of things to her basket and treats them like puppies. Her teats swell and sometimes milk is actually produced. The female will sometimes behave aggressively towards people or other animals, as if she is defending her young. Phantom pregnancies usually begin two months after a season and can last

a number of weeks. If it happens to a bitch once, it will often then occur after every season. If she suffers under it, sterilisation is the best solution, because continual phantom pregnancies increase the risk of womb or teat conditions. In the short term a hormone treatment is worth trying, perhaps also homeopathic medicines. Camphor spirit can give relief when teats are heavily swollen, but rubbing the teats with ice or a cold cloth (moisten and freeze) can also help relieve the pain. Feed the female less than usual, and make sure she gets enough attention and extra exercise.

Preparing to breed

If you do plan to breed a litter of puppies, you must first wait for your female to be physically and mentally full-grown. In any event you must let her first and second season pass. To mate a bitch, you need a male. You could simply let her out on the street and she will almost certainly quickly return home pregnant. But if you have a pure-bred Westie, then it certainly makes sense to mate her with the best possible candidate. Proceed with caution and especially remember that accompanying a bitch through pregnancy, birth and the first eight to twelve weeks

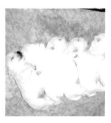

afterwards is a time-consuming affair. Never breed with a bitch that has congenital defects. The same goes for hyperactive, nervous and shy dogs. If your Westie does have a pedigree, then mate her with a dog that also has one. For more information, contact the breed association. You can also visit a dog show and look at the males present, and any offspring that may be there.

Pregnancy

It's often difficult to tell at first when a bitch is pregnant. Only after about four weeks can you feel the pups in her womb. She will now slowly get fatter and her behaviour will usually change. Her teats will swell during the last few weeks of pregnancy. The average pregnancy lasts 63 days, and costs her a lot of energy. In the beginning she is fed her normal

amount of food, but her nutritional needs increase in jumps during the second half of the pregnancy. Give her approximately fifteen percent more food each week from the fifth week on. The mother-to-be needs extra energy and proteins during this phase of her pregnancy.

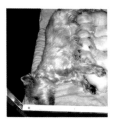

During the last weeks you can give her a concentrated food, rich in energy, such as dry puppy food. Divide this into several small portions per day, because she can no longer deal with large portions of food. Towards the end of the pregnancy, her energy needs can easily be one-and-a-half times more than usual.

After about seven weeks the mother will start to demonstrate nesting behaviour and to look for a place to give birth to her young. This might be her own basket or a special whelping box. This must be ready at least a week before the birth to give the mother time to get used to it. The basket or box should preferably be in a quiet place.

The birth

The average litter is between three and five puppies. The birth usually passes without problems. Of course, you must contact your vet immediately if you suspect a problem!

Suckling

weeks old. There are special puppy foods available that follow on well from the mother's milk and can easily be eaten with their milk teeth. Ideally, the puppies are fully weaned at an age of six or seven weeks, i.e. they no longer drink their mother's milk. The mother's milk production gradually stops and her food needs also drop. Within a couple of weeks after weaning, the mother should again be getting the same amount of food as before the pregnancy.

After birth, the mother starts to produce milk. The suckling period is very demanding. During the first three to four weeks the pups rely entirely on their mother's milk. During this time she needs extra food and fluids. This can be up to three or four times the normal amount. If she's producing too little milk, you can give both mother and her young special puppy milk. Here too, divide the high quantity of food the mother needs over several smaller portions. Again, choose a concentrated, high-energy, food and give her plenty of fresh drinking water, but not cow's milk, which can cause diarrhoea. You can give the puppies some supplemental solid food when they are three to four

Castration and sterilisation

As soon as you are sure your bitch should never bear a (new) litter, a vasectomy or sterilisation is the best solution. During sterilisation (in fact this is normal castration) the uterus is removed in an operation. The bitch no longer goes into season and can never become pregnant. The best age for a sterilisation is about eighteen months, when the bitch is more or less fully-grown. A male dog is usually only castrated for medical reasons or to correct undesirable sexual behaviour. During a castration the testicles are removed, which is a simple procedure and usually without complications. There is no special age for castration but, where possible, wait until the dog is fully-grown. Vasectomy is sufficient where it's only a case of making the dog infertile. In this case the dog keeps its sexual drive but can no longer reproduce.

Shows

Visiting a dog show is a pleasant experience for both dog and master, and for some dog-lovers it has become an intensive hobby.

They visit countless shows every year. Others find it nice to visit an exemption show with their dog just once. It's worth making the effort to visit an exemption show where a judge's experienced eyes will inspect your West Highland White Terrier and assess it for form, gait, condition and behaviour. The judge's report will teach you your dog's weak and strong points, which may help you when choosing a mate for breeding. You can also exchange experiences with other West Highland White Terrier owners. Official dog shows are only open to dogs with a pedigree

Ring training and club events
If you've never been to a dog show, you will probably be fumbling in the dark in terms of what

will be expected of you and your dog. Many West Highland White Terrier and general dog clubs organise so-called ring training courses for dogs going to a show for the first time. This training teaches you exactly what the judge will be looking for, and you can practice this together with your dog.

Open shows
All dog clubs organise dog shows. You must enter your dog in advance in a certain class. These meetings are usually small and friendly and are often the first acquaintance dog and master make with a "real" judge. This is an overwhelming experience for your dog - a lot of its contemporaries and a strange man or woman who fiddles around with it and peers into

its mouth. After a few times, your dog will know exactly what's expected of it and will happily go to the next club match.

Championship shows

Various championship shows take place during the course of the year with different prizes. These shows are much more strictly organised than club matches. Your dog must be registered in a certain class in advance and it will then be listed in a catalogue. On the day itself, the dog is usually kept on a bench until its turn comes up. During the judging in the ring, it's important that you show your dog at its best.

The judge examines each dog in turn. When all the dogs from that class have been judged, the best are selected and placed. After the judging has finished, all the winners of the same sex in the various classes compete for the Challange Certificate(3 Challenge certificates from different judges, and your West Highland White Terrier will be a Champion in the UK.) The best West Highland White Terrier in the eyes of the judge gets this award. Finally, the winners of each sex compete for the title of Best in Show.

Of course, your dog must look very smart for the show. The judge will not be impressed if its coat is not clean or is tangled, and its paws are dirty. Nails must be

clipped and teeth free of plaque. The dog must also be free of parasites and ailments. A bitch must not be in season and a male must be in possession of both testicles. Apart from those things, judges also hate badly brought-up, anxious or nervous dogs. Get in touch with your local dog club or the breed association if you want to know more about shows.

If you're planning to take your dog to a club match or in fact to any show, you need to be well prepared. Don't forget the following:

For yourself:
- Show documents if they have been sent to you
- Food and drink
- Clip for the catalogue number
- Chairs if an outside show

For your dog:
- Food and water bowls and food
- Dog blanket and perhaps a cushion
- Show lead
- A brush
- A benching chain and collar
- A trimming table
- Possibly some chalk for cleaning its coat.

Parasites

All dogs are vulnerable to various sorts of parasite. Parasites are tiny creatures that live at the expense of another animal. They feed on blood, skin and other body substances.

There are two main types. Internal parasites live within their host animal's body (tapeworm and roundworm) and external parasites live on the animal's exterior, usually in its coat (fleas and ticks), but also in its ears (ear mite).

Fleas

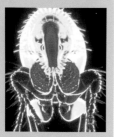

Flea

Fleas feed on a dog's blood. They cause not only itching and skin problems, but can also carry infections such as tapeworm. In large numbers they can cause anaemia and dogs can also become allergic to a flea's saliva, which can cause serious skin conditions. So it's important to treat your dog for fleas as effectively as possible, not just on the dog itself but also in its surroundings. For treatment on the animal, there are various medicines: drops for the neck and to put in its food, flea collars, long-life sprays and flea powders. There are various sprays in pet shops that can be used to eradicate fleas in the dog's immediate surroundings. Choose a spray that kills both adult fleas and their larvae. If your dog goes in your car, you should spray that too. Fleas can also affect other pets, so you should treat those too. When spraying a room, cover any aquarium or fishbowl. If the spray reaches the water, it can be fatal for your fish!

Your vet and pet shop have a wide range of flea treatments and can advise you on the subject.

Ticks

Ticks are small, spider-like parasites. They feed on the blood of the animal or person they've settled on. A tick looks like a tiny, grey-coloured leather bag with eight feet. When it has sucked itself full, it can easily be five to ten times its own size and is darker in colour.

Dogs usually fall victim to ticks in bushes, woods or long grass. Ticks cause not only irritation by their blood sucking but can also carry a number of serious diseases. This applies especially to the Mediterranean countries, which can be infested with blood parasites. In our country these diseases are fortunately less common. But Lyme disease, which can also affect humans, has reached our shores. Your vet can prescribe a special treatment if you're planning to take your dog to southern Europe. It is important to fight ticks as effectively as possible. Check your dog regularly, especially when it's been running free in woods and bushes. It can also wear an anti-tick collar.

Tick

Removing a tick is simple using a tick pincette. Grip the tick with the pincette as close to the dog's skin as possible and carefully pull it out. You can also grip the tick between your fingers and, using a turning movement, pull it carefully out. You must disinfect the spot where the tick had been using iodine to prevent infection. Never soak the tick in alcohol, ether or oil. In a shock reaction the tick may discharge the infected contents of its stomach into the dog's skin.

Worms

Dogs can suffer from various types of worm. The most common are tapeworm and roundworm. Tapeworm causes diarrhoea and poor condition. With a tapeworm infection you can sometimes find small pieces of the worm around the dog's anus or on its bed. In this case, the dog must be wormed. You should also check your dog for fleas, which carry the tapeworm infection.

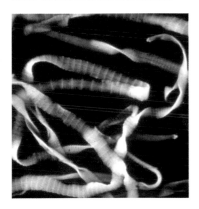

Tapeworm

Roundworm is a condition that reoccurs regularly. Puppies are often infected by their mother's milk. Your vet has medicines to prevent this. Roundworm causes problems (particularly in younger dogs), such as diarrhoea, loss of weight and stagnated growth. In serious cases the pup becomes thin, but with a swollen belly. It may vomit and you can then see the worms in its vomit. They are spaghetti-like tendrils.

A puppy must be treated for worms with a worm treatment every three months during its first year. Adult dogs should be treated every six months.

Roundworm

Your Westie's health

The space in this book is too limited to go into the medical ups and downs of the West Highland White Terrier.

However, we do want to briefly cover a number of diseases that occur more frequently with this breed than with other dogs.

Breed-specific diseases
C.M.O. (Cranio Manibular Osteopathy) is a condition of the jaws that appears between the 4th and 9th Month. The dog has swollen jaws, is in pain and can eat only with difficulty. This condition is now easily treated.

Legg Perthes (or Calvés disease)
This is a condition of the hip, which occurs in small breeds. The symptoms, a hot and painful hip joint, usually appear between 5 and 8 months and are accompanied by a lot of pain. Surgery usually offers the best results.

Patella Luxation
This is an abnormality of the knee ligaments and knee-cap. This causes dislocation of the knee and the dog can't walk properly and is in pain. Medicines or surgery can often help.

Skin conditions
In many cases, dogs with skin problems are sensitive to skin parasites, a so-called flea allergy. Food allergies may also be the cause in some cases. Treatments vary widely because so many factors can be involved and, in the past, results were poor. However, it seems that some vets are now getting results.

Cataracts
This eye condition causes a clouding of the retina. It can

appear in young animals and is passed on by both parents. If only a part of the retina is affected cataracts need not lead to total blindness, but unfortunately this is usually the consequence in most cases.

The West Highland White Terrier on the internet

A great deal of information can be found on the internet. A selection of websites with interesting details and links to other sites and pages is listed here. Sometimes pages move to another site or address. You can find more sites by using the available searchmachines.

www.thewesthighlandwhiteterrier-clubofengland.co.uk
The West Highland White Terrier Club of England. Here you may find more information on the standard of the breed, code of ethics, shows, breed information etc.

www.the-kennel-club.org.uk
The Kennel Club's primary objective is to promote, in every way, the general improvement of dogs. This site aims to provide you with information you may need to be a responsible pet owner and to help you keep your dog happy, safe and content.

www.k9-care.co.uk
The Self-Help site for dog owners. A beautiful website with tons of information on dogs. All you need to know about grooming, training, health care, buying a dog, travel and much more.

www.thedogscene.com/index.htm
The Dog Scene, this site is dedicated to pedigree dogs in the United Kingdom. Dog breeds, articles, shopping mall are a number of the issues you can find on this website.

www.pet-insurance-uk.me.uk
Find low cost pet insurance via this UK pet insurance directory.

www.pethealthcare.co.uk
At PEThealthcare.co.uk they believe that a healthy pet is a happy pet. Which is why they've brought together leading experts to create a comprehensive online source of pet care information.

www.onlinepetcare.co.uk
www.onlinepetcare.co.uk was launched in 2001 and contains information about and links to businesses and charities in the Midlands area involved in the care and purchasing of domestic animals.

http://champdogs.co.uk
Search the champ dogs database for kennels, stud dogs and litters.

http://dogtraining.co.uk
Your central resource for dog-training, boarding kennels & vets in the UK.

About Pets

- The Border Collie
- The Boxer
- The Cavalier King
  Charles Spaniel
- The Cocker Spaniel
- The Dalmatian
- The Dobermann
- The German Shepherd
- The Golden Retriever
- The Jack Russell Terrier
- The Labrador Retriever
- The Puppy
- The Rottweiler
- The Budgerigar
- The Canary
- The Parrot
- The Cockatiel
- The Lovebird
- The Cat
- The Kitten
- The Dwarf Hamster
- The Dwarf Rabbit
- The Ferret
- The Gerbil
- The Guinea Pig
- The Hamster
- The Mouse
- The Rabbit
- The Rat
- The Goldfish
- The Tropical Fish
- The Snake

Key features of the series are:
- Most affordable books
- Packed with hands-on
  information
- Well written by experts
- Easy to understand language
- Full colour original photography
- 70 to 110 photos
- All one needs to know to
  care well for their pet
- Trusted authors, veterinary
  consultants, breed and species
  expert authorities
- Appropriate for first time
  pet owners
- Interesting detailed information
  for pet professionals
- Title range includes books
  for advanced pet owners
  and breeders
- Includes useful addresses,
  veterinary data, breed standards.

about pets

Breeders' Clubs

Becoming a member of a breeders' club can be very useful for good advice and interesting activities. Contact the Kennel Club in case addresses or telephone-numbers have changed.

The Kennel Club
1 Clarges Street
London
W1J 8AB
UK
Tel: 0870 606 6750
Fax: 020 7518 1058
www.thekennelclub.org.uk/

The Scottish Kennel Club
Eskmills Park
Station Road
Musselborough EH21 7PQ
Tel: 0131 665 3920
Fax: 0131 653 6937
www.scottishkennelclub.org
email:
info@scottishkennelclub.org

**The Irish
Kennel Club LTD.**
Fottrell House, Harold's Cross
Bridge, Dublin 6W.
Ireland
Tel: (01) 4533300 - 4532309 -
4532310.
Fax (01) 4533237
email: ikenclub@indigo.ie
www.ikc.ie

**National Terrier Club of
the United Kingdom**
Secretary: Monica Shuttleworth
email:
monica.shuttleworth@ntlworld.com
www.nationalterrier.co.uk/

**The West Highland White
Terrier Club Of England**
Shirley Hooper
Three Ashes Cottage
North Cadbury
Yeovil BA22 7BU
email: yorsarwesties@aol.com
http://www.thewesthighlandwhit-
eterrierclubofengland.co.uk/

**The West Highland
White Terrier Club**
Secretary / Treasurer
Mrs B Wilson
Castleton Farm
Blair Road
Kilwinning
KA13 7QH
Tel: 01294 557259
email: bettywilson@care4free.net

**West Highland White
Terrier Club of Wales**
Sola Hurst
Dilkhuish Bungalow
Church Lane
Nantgarw CF15 7TQ
Tel: 01443 841743
email:
secretary@whwtclubofwales.co.uk
www.welshclub.dog-lovers.org.uk/

**North of Ireland West Highland
White Terrier Club.**
Sec. Mrs M Johnston.
Tel: 01662 841618
email:
GlenveaghWesties@aol.com
http://www.northofirelandwesthig
hlandwhiteterrierclub.co.uk/

**Southern West Highland White
Terrier Club**
Sec. Mr J Griffin.
Tel: 01562 777266
http://www.southernwesthigh-
landwhiteterrierclub.co.uk/

**West Highland White Terrier
Club**
Sec. Mr McLean.
Tel: 01875 813909

The West Highland White Terrier

Name:	West Highland White Terrier
FCI Classification:	Breed group 3 - Terriers
Origin:	Scotland
Original tasks:	Hunting of pests, especially underground
Shoulder height:	Approx. 28 cm (11 inches)
Average life expectancy:	10 – 14 years

the **West Highland White Terrier**